D1530654

fresh from the farmer's market

spring

fresh from the farmer's market

spring

RYLAND
PETERS
& SMALL

cooking with Alastair Hendy

photography by David Loftus

First published in Great Britain in 1999
by Ryland Peters & Small
Cavendish House,
51–55 Mortimer Street,
London W1N 7TD

Text © Alastair Hendy 1999
Design and photographs
© Ryland Peters & Small 1999

Printed and bound in China

ISBN 1 900518 95 3

A CIP record for this book is available from the
British Library

Acknowledgements
My thanks to Egg, of Kinnerton Street, Belgravia,
London, who were so generous in lending
beautiful bowls for photography, and Kara Kara,
of Tokyo and Pond Place, South Kensington in
London, for Japanese ceramics and other props.

Notes
All spoon measurements are level unless
specified otherwise.
Ovens should be preheated to the specified
temperature. If using a fan-assisted oven,
cooking times should be reduced according to
the manufacturer's instructions.
Specialist Asian ingredients are available in
large supermarkets, Thai, Chinese, Japanese,
Vietnamese, and other Asian stores.

Designer
Robin Rout
Editor
Elsa Petersen-Schepelern
Editorial Assistant
Maddalena Bastianelli
Publishing Director
Anne Ryland
Production
Patricia Harrington

Stylist and
Food Stylist
Alastair Hendy
Cooking Assistant
Kate Habershon
Photographer's Assistant
Tara Fisher
Author Photograph
David Loftus

contents

Food isn't just about cooking. It's also about appreciating quality produce—the ruby red of rhubarb, the sensuous curve of the buds on a bunch of chives, the fresh aniseed aroma of chopped dill. Buying vegetables in season is the key to good cooking, and spring is the best time for the ingredients in this book; asparagus, spring greens, soft leaf herbs, peas, and rhubarb. It's all about tender leaves and shoots, bright-tasting pods, crisp stems, clean flavors, sweet textures, and garden flavors in full force.

No mucking about in the kitchen with complicated sauces. No fretting over too many weights and measures. Cooking now is about spontaneity: a freedom to cook without getting bogged down with complicated methods and difficult procedures. A bundle of this and a handful of that is the way we like to cook.

A knife, a chopping board, and a couple of pans is generally all you need. Flavors are fresh and should be kept that way, so cooking times are short. Creating food is also about care and love, and this will sometimes involve extra time and attention, such as creating a good stock or slow-cooking a beautiful ham. Enjoy your ingredients. Cooking should be therapeutic—a way to unwind, not wind up. Throughout, I've suggested variations within the recipes: different ways of combining parts of recipes with other ingredients— there to spark your own ideas or develop your favorite dishes. Often some things in a recipe aren't available when you go to the market. Rather than hunt high and low (which most of us haven't got time for), buy something else that catches your eye. Try it out. Follow the season, buy what's plentiful, and you can't go wrong.

Asparagus has mystery, an aristocratic air. It's a luxury, a privilege—not because it's expensive (unless of course you buy it out of season), but because it's at its peak for such a short time, mid to late spring. Resist the temptation to buy it out of season, and each spring your first taste of these tender spears will remain special. Asparagus comes in various colors from deep green to greeny-pink (known as green); purple and white (known as purple); and white with a hint of pink and a pastel purple head (known as white). I think green asparagus has the finest flavor although in Northern Europe, white is the most popular.

Cook green asparagus as simply as possible—steamed, boiled, roasted, or char-broiled—and with just a touch of crunch remaining. White asparagus on the other hand is better well-cooked—soft and without crunch. This is also the one variety that should always be peeled—otherwise it's rather stringy. Cooked properly, white asparagus has a beautiful mellow-tasting stem and is delicious with egg and creamy sauces, as well as the salty flavors of salmon roe, caviar, shrimp, crab, or ham.

Asparagus also comes in various shapes and sizes: sprue or wild asparagus is also known in the trade as "grass," short for "sparrow grass," and has wispy, wiry stems. Another wild asparagus, which is also called Thai asparagus, is pale green with thick chive-like stems tipped with perfect fat buds. Both need a minimum amount of cooking—the latter a mere blanching.

So, is there still mystery to asparagus? Yes, because we want it so—to keep it special. Someone, somewhere, is doing an excellent asparagus PR job.

aragus

Asparagus brunch with prosciutto toasts

The traditional way to cook asparagus is to stand the bundle upright in a tall saucepan and simmer in an inch of water. However, you'll need a special pan: instead, simmer the spears in salted water for a few minutes in an ordinary pan, or steam in a metal or bamboo steamer.

4 large eggs

1 bundle green asparagus (about 20 spears)

sea salt and cracked black pepper

butter, for brushing

Prosciutto toast:

4–8 slices white or brown bread, toasted

butter, for spreading

4–8 slices finely cut prosciutto ham

Serves 4

1

To cook soft-boiled eggs, prick the blunt ends to prevent cracking, put into a saucepan of cold water and bring to a boil. When the water reaches boiling point, set the timer for 4 minutes for soft eggs, 5 for harder yolks. Put into egg cups set on 4 dinner plates.

2

To prepare the asparagus, steam for a few minutes (or simmer in salted water) until tender but still crisp—test with the point of a knife. Remove from the steamer, brush with melted butter, and divide between the dinner plates.

3

Toast the bread, spread with butter, trim the crusts, and cut into 2–3 lengths. Wrap with prosciutto and add to the plates. Serve with sea salt and freshly ground black pepper.

4

To eat, dip the prosciutto toasts and the asparagus tips into the egg.

Asparagus soup

with water spinach and tamarind

The asparagus in Western soups is boiled and puréed: in this easier Eastern version it's lightly blanched, and remains packed with nutrients.

5 cups clear light chicken stock, or 1 chicken stock cube dissolved in 5 cups hot water

1 tablespoon fish sauce*

3 teaspoons sugar

1 small hot chile, finely sliced

1 inch fresh ginger, finely sliced

2 stalks lemongrass, trimmed and smashed with a rolling pin

1 teaspoon tamarind paste*

1 bundle young asparagus tips, sprue, or wild asparagus

1 small bunch water spinach (*ong choi*), other Oriental leaves, baby spinach leaves, or watercress, trimmed of any tough stems*

4 scallions, chopped

juice of ½ lime

Crispy shallots (optional):

6 shallots, finely sliced

a pinch of salt

vegetable oil, for cooking

Serves 4

Note: *Bottled fish sauce, tamarind paste, and other Oriental ingredients such as water spinach and Chinese leaves are sold in Asian shops.*

1

Put the stock, fish sauce, sugar, chile, ginger, lemongrass, and tamarind paste in a saucepan, bring to a boil, reduce the heat, and simmer for about 20 minutes.

2

Bring a large saucepan of salted water to a boil, plunge in the asparagus, return to a boil, simmer for 1 minute, then drain, rinse in cold water, and transfer to a bowl of ice water.

3

To make the crispy shallots, if using, put in a bowl and toss with salt. Heat the vegetable oil in a heavy-based skillet, add the shallots, and sauté until dark brown and crisp.

4

Divide the blanched asparagus, water spinach, and scallions between 4 small soup bowls. Reheat the stock if necessary, add the lime juice, then strain over the ingredients in the bowls, top with the crispy shallots, and serve.

Variations:

Add other ingredients such as cooked shrimp, poached chicken, wide rice noodles, or tofu.

13

Asparagus tips
roasted with lemon-soy butter

A bundle of asparagus tips has charm: it's a shame it has to be dismantled before cooking and serving, so tie it back together again to serve. An even more interesting variation is Thai asparagus—long thin stems with unopened buds on the end—or sprue, the baby shoots of asparagus, shown below.

1 bundle asparagus tips, with any tough ends trimmed and discarded

sea salt and freshly ground black pepper

olive oil, for brushing

long garlic chives, for tying (optional)

Lemon-soy butter:

⅔ cup unsalted butter

2 stalks lemongrass, trimmed, outer layers discarded, inside layers finely sliced

1 small hot chile, cored and finely chopped

1 garlic clove, crushed

2 tablespoons dark soy sauce

juice of ½ lemon

Serves 4

Variations:

Char-grill or oven-roast scallops in the shell, spoon the lemon-soy butter into the shell, then serve with poached or roasted asparagus tips.

Serve roasted asparagus tips with Parmesan cheese or poached egg.

1

To make the lemon-soy butter, melt the butter in a saucepan then pour carefully into a clean saucepan, leaving the milk solids behind. Add the lemongrass, chile, and garlic to the clarified butter and gently warm through for 10 minutes.

2

Arrange the asparagus across a roasting pan, sprinkle with salt and pepper, and brush with olive oil. Roast in a preheated oven at 400°F for 6 minutes.

3

Remove from the oven, tie into a bundle with garlic chives, if using, and set the bundle upright on a serving plate.

4

Mix the flavored butter with the soy sauce and lemon juice and serve separately or spoon it around the asparagus. To eat, dip the spears into the lemon-soy butter and eat with your fingers.

White asparagus

with salmon caviar hollandaise

White asparagus is the most popular variety in much of Northern Europe, especially Germany. We have used a very slim kind here, but it also grows very large, fat, and juicy. It also tends to have a very stringy skin, so peel it with a vegetable peeler. It has a refined, pale flavor and needs something salty like salmon eggs or caviar to show it off.

2 bundles white asparagus, woody ends trimmed if necessary

1 cup unsalted butter

1 shallot, finely chopped

½ cup white wine

2 egg yolks

juice of ½ lemon

4 oz. salmon caviar (keta)

salt and freshly ground white pepper

Serves 4

Variations:

Serve poached white asparagus with a ham salad.

Omit the salmon caviar and add chopped chives or other herbs to the hollandaise.

1

Peel the asparagus stalks with a vegetable peeler.

2

Melt the butter in a small saucepan and skim off the froth. Decant into a clean pan, discarding the milky liquid at the bottom. Reheat.

3

Put the chopped shallot and wine into a small saucepan, bring to a boil and reduce to about 2 tablespoons. Strain and reserve the liquid, discarding the solids.

4

Cook the asparagus in salted simmering water for 8 minutes or less for *al dente*. Drain and set aside in a warm place, covered.

5

Place a heatproof bowl over a saucepan of simmering water. Put the egg yolks in the bowl and slowly beat in the strained wine, beating until the mixture thickens. Slowly, while still beating, add the reheated clarified butter in a thin, steady stream. Do not overheat the eggs, or the mixture will curdle.

6

Add salt and pepper to taste, then stir in the lemon juice and the salmon caviar. Divide between 4 small dipping bowls and serve with the asparagus. Alternatively, serve the caviar separately.

Asparagus phyllo tart with spinach

Asparagus might have been specially made for the tart treatment—use long spears for a square pan or short ones for a rectangular pan.

1 lb. phyllo or shortcrust pastry

1 bunch spinach, about 20 large leaves, washed and trimmed

1 bundle asparagus (about 15 long spears or 20 short), ends trimmed

2 large potatoes, sliced

1¾ cups grated Gruyère cheese

½ teaspoon freshly grated nutmeg

3 eggs, lightly beaten (reserve a spoonful for glazing the pastry)

1 cup heavy cream

sea salt and freshly ground black pepper

olive oil, for poaching

To serve:

4 oz. Parmesan cheese, in the piece, shaved with a vegetable peeler

a small handful of chives

Serves 4

1

Roll out the pastry and line a 9-inch square pie pan or 14 x 4 inch rectangular pan. Prick the base and chill.

2

Plunge the spinach into a saucepan of boiling water, remove immediately with a slotted spoon, and refresh in a bowl of iced water. Drain and pat dry with paper towels. Do the same with the asparagus.

3

Put the potato slices in a saucepan, cover with olive oil, heat gently, then poach without browning until tender. Remove, then strain and reserve the oil for another use.

4

To assemble the tart, arrange a layer of cooked potato in the bottom of the pastry-lined pan. Season lightly with salt, pepper, and nutmeg. Add a layer of spinach and season again. Add the Gruyère and a second layer of potatoes and spinach, seasoning each one.

5

Beat the eggs and cream in a pitcher or bowl, then pour over the potatoes and spinach. Arrange a line of cooked asparagus over the top of the tart. Brush the pastry with the reserved egg.

6

Bake in a preheated oven at 350°F for 30–35 minutes. Half way through the cooking time, cover the asparagus, but not the pastry edge, with a sheet of foil or buttered parchment paper. When the center of the tart is just set, remove it from the oven and serve with shavings of Parmesan and chives.

Salmon fish fingers

with asparagus, spring peas, and mustard-mint butter

This asparagus mixture is wonderful on its own as an appetizer—or with fish, meat, or poultry as an entrée. Vary the ingredients according to whatever is fresh and exciting at the market.

20 asparagus tips

4 small green or yellow zucchini, halved

8 oz. mixed spring peas or beans

4 tablespoons butter

1 tablespoon whole-grain mustard

chopped fresh mint and chives, to serve

Fish fingers:

4 salmon fillets (6 oz. each)

½ cup couscous

1 garlic clove, crushed

grated zest of 1 lemon

1 teaspoon paprika

1 teaspoon ground cumin

1 teaspoon ground coriander

1 teaspoon ground ginger

flour, for dusting

1 egg, lightly beaten

salt and pepper

butter and olive oil, for cooking

Serves 4

1

To make the fish fingers, pat the salmon dry with paper towels. Put the couscous in a bowl, add boiling water until just covered, then set aside for 5 minutes until doubled in size. Fluff up with a fork, leave 5 minutes more, then fluff up again. Spread out on a wide plate and let dry for 10 minutes. Mix with the garlic, lemon zest, paprika, cumin, coriander, ginger, salt, and pepper. Dip the fish in flour, then in beaten egg, then in the couscous mixture—pat on extra. Chill for 2 minutes.

2

Blanch the asparagus, zucchini, and beans, if using, in boiling salted water for 1–2 minutes. Add the sugar snaps or snowpeas, if using, and blanch for 1 minute more.

3

Heat the butter and oil in a skillet, add the fish, and sauté gently for 2 minutes on each side. Remove and drain on paper towels.

4

Heat the butter and mustard in a large shallow skillet or wok, add the drained vegetables, and toss well. Heat through for about 1 minute, then toss in the mint.

5

To serve, slice each fillet lengthwise to make 2 "fingers." Put 2 pieces of fish on each plate, and pile the mustard buttered vegetables on top. Sprinkle with chives and serve.

Aren't spring greens just cabbages? Yes—and much more. They include all those fresh, tender, sweet leaves that fill the shelves from early spring. The garden, too, is bursting into serious action: stems and leaves shoot forth on a mad photosynthetic high. Everything feels good and fresh. Take a look at these new shoots, these vegetable infants—all the bundles, soft hearts, and bags of leaves on offer. Spring cabbage is special. It's not your everyday cabbage, but a sweet young thing with an open heart of sensuous leaves packed with flavor. Handled with care and simply cooked, these cabbages not only look good, they taste very good. Torn or chopped, blanched, then wilted with butter—that is all the cooking they need.

spring

Oriental greens include the white stubby stems and crinkly dark leaves of bok choy, the crunchy stems and soft leaves of water spinach, hot mustard cabbage hearts, tight bundles of dark green watercress, and the delicate pink-hearted leaves of amaranth. All can be used in stir-fries, soups, or salads.

Other softer baby leaves of chard, mizuna, and even curly kale are delicious tossed into warm salad or in toasted sandwiches. Brussels plants are usually grown for their sprouts and turnips for their roots—but the tender tops of both plants are as good, if not better, than shoot or root. Spring greens have never looked or tasted so wonderful, so just buy what looks fresh and attractive and you can't go wrong.

greens

Spring cabbage packages
with poached chicken, peanuts, herbs, and chopped lime

Raw cabbage leaves are a fresh, peppery wrapping for a filling with a decidedly Southeast Asian flavor—and make excellent party food.

1 small chicken, about 2½ lb.

8 small shallots, preferably Thai or Chinese

2½ inches fresh ginger, peeled and halved

3 garlic cloves, 2 whole, 1 crushed

1¼ cups Shaohsing (rice wine)

1 tablespoon fish sauce

2 tablespoons rice vinegar

1 tablespoon superfine sugar

2 small hot chiles, finely sliced

2 limes

1 spring cabbage, outer dark leaves only, washed

2 stems green peppercorns, coarsely chopped (optional)

a handful of roasted salted peanuts, lightly crushed, about 4 tablespoons

herb sprigs, such as basil, mint, and cilantro

sea salt

Serves 4

1

Put the chicken in a large saucepan, add salt, pour in water to cover, and bring to a boil. Skim off any foam. Add 4 shallots, half the ginger, and 2 whole garlic cloves. Reduce the heat, cover, and simmer for 40 minutes. Turn off the heat and let cool in the stock.

2

Lift the chicken from the stock. Discard all the skin and bones, then tear the meat into thick shreds and place in a bowl. Strain the chicken poaching stock and reserve for another use, freezing if necessary.

3

Put the rice wine, fish sauce, vinegar, and sugar in a bowl and mix until the sugar is fully dissolved. Add the crushed garlic, chiles, and the juice of 1 lime. Stir well, then pour over the chicken and chill for 2 hours or overnight. Remove the chicken from the marinade before serving.

4

Using scissors, remove and discard the midrib from each cabbage leaf, then cut the leaves into rough square shapes. Chop the remaining shallots lengthwise and finely slice the remaining ginger. Chop the remaining lime into small dice, including the rind.

5

Arrange all the prepared ingredients in piles or in bowls, add a little of each to a square of cabbage, roll up, and eat.

Spinach and sorrel gnocchi

If you don't have any sorrel available, use all spinach leaves instead. The traditional way of making gnocchi is by rolling pieces of dough off the end of a fork. This becomes easier after you've had a little bit of practice, but I like this version—it's much easier, and I think the little cushions of spinach-flavoured dough look much prettier as well!

5 oz. baby spinach and sorrel leaves, well washed

1¾ cups ricotta cheese, drained of excess whey

3 egg yolks

a pinch of ground allspice

1 oz. fresh Parmesan cheese, grated

⅔ cup all-purpose flour

salt and freshly ground black pepper

Basil oil:

a small bunch of basil, coarsely chopped

6 tablespoons fruity virgin olive oil

Serves 4

1

To blanch the spinach and sorrel, plunge into boiling salted water for 2 minutes. Drain and squeeze dry in a cloth. Chop finely.

2

Put in a bowl with the ricotta, eggs, allspice, Parmesan, flour, salt, and pepper, and work to a firm dough, adding extra flour if necessary.

3

Roll the dough into a long sausage shape, 1 inch thick. Cut into segments about 1 inch long and put on a lightly floured surface.

4

Mix the basil and oil in a small pitcher.

5

Bring a large saucepan of salted water to a boil, add the prepared gnocchi, and cook for about 2–3 minutes. Drain, divide between 4 heated plates or bowls, and dress with basil oil and freshly ground black pepper.

Bacon-wrapped monkfish
with wilted Brussels tops and horseradish picada

Brussels sprouts grow on a tall plant, with the small round sprouts growing tightly up the stem, topped by a crown of loose leaves. These leaves are one of the best things about sprouts—and if you aren't usually a fan, they will be a revelation. Use ordinary spring cabbage if you can't find them.

4 monkfish fillets, about 1½ lb. in total

8 slices bacon

4 Brussels tops, coarse stems removed

1 tablespoon balsamic vinegar

2 tablespoons olive oil, plus extra for brushing

salt and freshly ground black pepper

Horseradish picada:

⅓ cup olive oil, or to taste

⅓ cup skinned hazelnuts*

⅓ cup skinned almonds*

1 thick slice white bread

½ tablespoon sherry vinegar

2 tablespoons raisins, soaked in sherry vinegar

3 tablespoons creamed horseradish

salt and freshly ground black pepper

Serves 4

Note: To skin nuts, soak for a few minutes in boiling water, then pop them out of their brown skins (almonds) or wrap them in a cloth and rub them off (hazelnuts).

1

To make the picada, heat 1 tablespoon of the oil in a skillet, add the nuts and gently sauté until lightly browned. Remove, and sauté the bread in the same oil. Put the nuts, bread, salt, and pepper in a food processor and blend to a paste. With the motor running, slowly add olive oil in a thin stream until the paste becomes a thick sauce. Stir in vinegar to taste, then add the raisins and horseradish. Set aside.

2

Lightly sprinkle the monkfish with salt and pepper, wrap each piece in 2 bacon slices, and put into a roasting pan. Brush the wrapped fish with olive oil and put the pan on top of the stove. Cook over a high heat until lightly brown all over. Transfer to a preheated oven and roast at 425°F for 8–10 minutes. Remove from the oven. If the bacon has not crisped, brown under a hot broiler.

3

Half fill a wok with water, then add salt and pepper. Bring to a boil then add the prepared Brussels tops and blanch for 1 minute. Drain off the water, then add the vinegar and 2 tablespoons olive oil, more salt and pepper, and stir-fry for a further 1 minute.

4

Divide the wilted Brussels tops between 4 wide, shallow bowls. Slice each piece of monkfish into 4 and place on top of the wilted leaves. Serve with a spoonful of picada.

Honeyed duck

with baby chard, cilantro, and mustard seed mayo in ciabatta

Perhaps the most welcome kinds of spring green are the mini shoots of salad leaves, such as baby chard, mizuna, frisée, arugula, or other interesting shoots and leaves. These delicious salad packages make great party food—use small pita breads, toast, or these hollowed out ciabatta rolls cut in half. Alternatively, serve as a main course salad of duck and salad leaves, topped with mustard seed mayonnaise. Serve the ciabatta as an accompaniment.

1 large duck breast

1 teaspoon five-spice powder

1 tablespoon honey

1 tablespoon light soy sauce

1 teaspoon cumin seeds

2 teaspoons sesame seeds, toasted in a dry skillet

½ tablespoon whole-grain mustard

2 tablespoons mayonnaise

a handful of baby chard leaves or other robust salad leaves

a handful of mizuna or frisée leaves

a handful of cilantro stems, coarsely chopped

a handful of scallions, sliced lengthwise into strips

ciabatta rolls, halved and hollowed, pitta breads, or buttered toast

sea salt and freshly ground black pepper

Serves 4

1

Score fine cuts across the skin of the duck and rub with salt and five-spice powder. Pour over the honey and soy sauce, rub in, and marinate for 1–2 hours in the refrigerator.

2

Put the duck breast, skin side down, in a preheated heavy-based skillet, and char-grill for 4 minutes. Turn it over and cook for a further 4–5 minutes. The skin will look charred but won't taste burnt: the flesh should be pink. Let it rest for 10 minutes, then cut crosswise into thin slices.

3

Mix the cumin seeds, sesame seeds, and mustard with the mayonnaise. Coat the inside of the breads with the mixture and stuff with remaining ingredients.

Anise braised pork

with Chinese mustard cabbage

Mustard cabbage takes you by surprise: the sensuous leaves hide a mustardy fire. Sold by Chinese grocers, these stems or large hearts of translucent yellow green leaves look a bit like an elongated iceberg lettuce. Don't worry about the quantity of soy sauce—it's for poaching, not eating, and you can freeze it to use again.

2 lb. boned pork leg

2 teaspoons five-spice powder

3 tablespoons peanut oil

1 bottle soy sauce (1¾ cups)

6 small pink shallots, or 1–2 large

2 inches fresh ginger, sliced

3 garlic cloves, sliced

2 small fresh whole red chiles

4 tablespoons mirin (rice wine)

1 tablespoon honey

4 whole star anise

1 Chinese mustard cabbage (*dai gai choi*) or other Chinese greens

sea salt

Serves 4

1

Score the pork rind with diagonal cuts. Put in a colander and pour over a pitcher of boiling water. Pat dry with paper towels. Rub a little salt and five-spice powder into the scored skin. Heat 2 tablespoons of the oil in a skillet, add the pork, skin side down, and sauté until lightly scorched. Add 3 tablespoons soy sauce and reduce until caramelized. Transfer the pork to a casserole or sand pot.

2

Heat the remaining oil in the skillet, add the shallots, ginger, garlic, and chiles, and sauté until browned. Add the mirin, honey, star anise, the remaining soy sauce, and 2¾ cups water. Stir to dissolve the honey. Transfer to the casserole.

3

Bring to a boil, cover, turn the heat to low, and simmer gently for 2–2½ hours until meltingly tender. Put the mustard cabbage leaves around the pork and braise for 5 minutes more.

4

Slice the pork and serve with the cabbage and a few spoonfuls of the casserole juices.

Stir-fried spring greens

with sukiyaki-style beef and fluffy rice

Spring greens might have been created especially for the stir-fry treatment. It keeps their crunch, vitamins, and brilliant color like no other cooking method. Rice, by the way, is best measured by volume, not weight.

2¾ cups short-grain rice, washed well in cold water

5 tablespoons sugar

½ cup rice vinegar

1 tablespoon salt

1 inch fresh ginger, finely sliced

3 whole small red fresh chiles

1 lb. beef filet or lean sirloin, cut into ⅛-inch slices

2 tablespoons dark soy sauce

2 tablespoons sake or vodka

2 tablespoons mirin (rice wine) or dry sherry

a bunch of spring greens, Chinese leaves, or other greens, trimmed of tough ribs and stems

1 garlic clove, sliced

2 tablespoons peanut oil mixed with 2 tablespoons sesame oil, for stir-frying

toasted sesame seeds, to serve (optional)

Serves 4

1

Put the rice in a saucepan with 3⅔ cups water and cover with a lid. Bring slowly to a boil and boil for 3 minutes. Reduce the heat to low and simmer for 8 minutes. Turn off the heat and leave the rice (with lid on) for a further 10 minutes.

2

Put the sugar, vinegar, and salt in a saucepan, bring to a boil, then let cool. Transfer the rice to a large bowl, pour over the dressing and fold through with a large spoon or wooden spatula. Cover with a cloth.

3

Heat the oil in a wok or large skillet, add the ginger and chiles, then add the beef and sear on both sides. Add the soy sauce, sake and mirin and reduce to a sticky paste.

4

Divide the rice between serving bowls and top with the beef. Add the greens and garlic to the wok and stir-fry with a drop of peanut and sesame oil. Pile into the bowls or serve separately, sprinkled with toasted sesame seeds, if using.

Peas need no introduction: we were all practically weaned on them. But we've forgotten, now we're all grown up, just how good they taste. Fresh from the pod, they're cellulose-sweet, rich in potassium, phosphorus, and vitamins.

Little devils to eat, they run all over the plate and after the chase you can't stick many on your fork. But they're worth it. Every mouthful keeps you coming back to chase a few more—down to the last caught and pronged pea on the plate. Peas from pods picked from the garden the same day barely need cooking.

Pods of unshelled peas are only available in spring—look for shiny, plump pods (a few minor blemishes here or there won't affect the peas inside). The peas themselves should be small—the larger ones are older and will taste floury.

A plate of buttered peas (with mint if you like) go hand-in-hand with so many of our best-loved meals. From the robust and homely—like roast ham, sausages and mashed potatoes, fish fingers, chicken pie, or steak and kidney pie—to the more refined heights of peas with basil and olive oil, peas braised with lettuce hearts and bacon, and delicate purées served with seared scallops, broiled artichoke hearts, or asparagus.

It's not just the peas we eat. Other parts of the plant are good too—like the flat pods of snowpeas, known in France as *mangetout*—"eat-all." Snowpea is a more romantic name, probably the result of their being harvested through winter and spring. They need only brief blanching, steaming, or stir-frying, as do sugar snaps (another sweet eat-all pod), to retain their goodness, delightful crunch, and vivid spring green color.

Pea shoots are the tender growing tips of snowpea plants, and need no cooking. These little leaves and tendrils bring a sweet taste to a salad, and look charming too. They are also good in stir-fries or Chinese soups, and so are commonly sold in Chinese markets (as *dau mui*).

So—peas are a handy lot. Shelling takes time, but if you listen to the radio or just daydream, podding is repetitive therapy. Wouldn't you prefer your peas from their natural pod rather than frozen and out of a plastic bag?

peas

Pea quiche

Classic quiche, with eggs, cream, and salty bacon. You can't beat it! Add fresh cooked peas and nothing could be easier, or taste and look so good— one course in a slice. Serve plain, or top with more peas and a sprig of mint.

1 pack frozen shortcrust pastry, about 1 lb., thawed

1 tablespoon olive oil

3 oz. pancetta or bacon lardons

1 garlic clove, finely chopped

2½ cups cooked green peas

1 tablespoon torn fresh tarragon or basil

4 eggs, beaten (retain a spoonful for brushing the pastry)

¾ cup heavy cream

sea salt and freshly ground black pepper

To serve (optional):

about 1 cup shelled peas, cooked

sprigs of mint or basil

Serves 4

1

Roll out the pastry and use to line the base and sides of a deep 6-inch springform or loose-based cake pan. Prick the base of the pastry and chill.

2

Heat the oil in a skillet, add the pancetta or bacon, sauté until crisp, then stir in the garlic. Sprinkle the crispy mixture over the base of the pastry, fill the pastry shell with peas, then sprinkle with tarragon or basil.

3

Put the eggs, cream, salt, and pepper in a bowl, beat well, then pour the mixture into the pie shell. Brush the pastry with the reserved egg and cover loosely with foil.

4

Bake in a preheated oven at 400°F for about 45 minutes or until set. Check after 20 minutes: if the top is browning, cover the top of the quiche with foil and move to the bottom shelf of the oven. Serve warm as is, or topped with a pile of peas and sprigs of mint or basil.

Variations:

Use ¾ cup ricotta instead of cream, and add layers of blanched sliced zucchini.

Indian yellow dhaal

with peas, coconut, and paneer

This soupy pea dhaal, or lentil stew, is made with coconut milk and paneer, the delicious North Indian curd cheese—use mozzarella if you can't find it. This recipe tastes even better if made the day before, so the flavor of the chiles, leaves, and spices fully penetrate the split peas and cheese.

⅓ cup yellow split peas, or channa dhaal, washed in several changes of cold water

2 teaspoons ground coriander

2 teaspoons cumin seeds

1 teaspoon fenugreek seeds

1 inch cinnamon stick

4 small dried chiles

6 small shallots, sliced

1 teaspoon ground turmeric

2 sprigs curry leaves* (optional)

1¼ cups shelled green peas

1¾ cups coconut milk

1 cup paneer cheese* or mozzarella, cubed

1 teaspoon mustard seeds

salt and pepper

vegetable oil, for frying

hot paprika, for sprinkling

1 package pappadams* (or potato chips), to serve

Serves 4

Note: available from Asian stores

1

Put the yellow split peas in a saucepan with 2¾ cups water, bring to a boil, reduce the heat, and simmer for about 50 minutes, skimming off the froth from time to time.

2

Grind the coriander, cumin, fenugreek, cinnamon, and 1 dried chile in a spice mill or coffee grinder. Heat 2 tablespoons of the oil in a skillet, add the shallots, and sauté until soft. Stir in the ground spice mixture and turmeric and cook until the shallots are golden-brown.

3

Transfer to the saucepan of split pea dhaal, add 1 sprig of curry leaves, if using. Season well, and simmer for 10 minutes. Stir in the peas, coconut milk, and paneer, then gently simmer the dhaal for 15 minutes—add extra water if the mixture has thickened too much (it should remain soupy).

4

Heat 2 tablespoons of the vegetable oil in a small skillet, add the mustard seeds, the remaining chiles and curry leaves, and sauté for a few seconds. Add to the dhaal and serve in 1 large bowl or divide between 4 small bowls.

5

If using pappadams, wipe out the small pan, pour in 1 inch depth of vegetable oil and heat until a small piece of pappadam browns in 30 seconds. Fry the pappadams, one by one, until crisp. Remove, drain, sprinkle with hot paprika, and serve with the dhaal.

Steamed sea bass

with snowpeas and black beans

Slice some ginger, garlic, and scallions, set the fish on its bed of snowpeas and black beans, and you're there—10 minutes is all it takes. If you're not keen on handling (or for that matter seeing) a whole fish—with head, fins, tail, and all—on your table, then ask your fishmonger to fillet it for you then put the two fillets together before cooking.

1 whole sea bass (about 2 lb.), cleaned, scaled, and washed

1 garlic clove, sliced

2 inches fresh ginger, finely sliced

a handful of snowpeas

2 tablespoons whole black beans (drained if in brine)

4 scallions, halved crosswise, then lengthwise

2 teaspoons sesame oil

sea salt and crushed Szechuan peppercorns or black pepper

sprigs of cilantro or Thai basil leaves, to serve

Ginger dipping sauce:

4 tablespoons soy sauce

1 inch fresh ginger, grated

Serves 4

1
Sprinkle the fish inside and out with salt and pepper and tuck half the garlic and ginger into the cavity.

2
Arrange the snowpeas down one side of a piece of parchment paper, sprinkle over the black beans, and place the fish on top. Sprinkle with the scallions, the remaining ginger and garlic, and the sesame oil.

3
Fold over the paper to enclose the fish and crease the edges together. Place in a steamer or oven preheated to 400°F, and cook for 10 minutes.

4
Mix the dipping sauce ingredients in a small bowl.

5
Open the package, sprinkle the fish with herbs, and serve with the dipping sauce.

Fish fillets in beer batter

with pea purée and mint vinaigrette

Delicious pea purée is sometimes made from dried peas, but here I have made it with fresh spring peas. I used monkfish, a cartilaginous fish which has no fine bones and so is easy to eat. If you can't find one, substitute another fish—cod or flounder would be good—but remove any pin bones.

2 lb. fish fillets, such as monkfish, skate, cod or flounder, cut into 4 pieces

sea salt

sunflower or vegetable oil, for deep-frying

Beer batter:

1⅓ cups all-purpose flour, plus extra to dust

½ teaspoon sea salt

2 teaspoons baking powder

1 cup beer

2 egg whites

Pea purée:

2 tablespoons sweet butter

1 small onion, chopped

1 thick slice of bacon

2 cups shelled peas

Mint vinaigrette:

½ teaspoon sugar

leaves from 1 bunch mint, chopped

4 tablespoons virgin olive oil

2 tablespoons lemon juice

1 tablespoon balsamic vinegar

sea salt and freshly ground black pepper

Serves 4

1

To make the batter, sieve the flour, salt, and baking powder in a bowl. Stir in the beer and set aside for 30 minutes. Beat the egg whites to soft peak stage and mix in just before using.

2

To make the pea purée, melt the butter in a saucepan, add the onion, and cook gently until softened and translucent, about 5–10 minutes. Add the bacon and peas and cover with water (do not salt). Bring to a boil, reduce the heat, and simmer for 10 minutes. Discard the bacon, put the peas in a food processor, add salt and pepper to taste, then work to a purée. Set aside to keep warm.

3

To make the mint vinaigrette, beat the sugar, mint, oil, lemon juice, vinegar, salt, and pepper in a pitcher or bowl.

4

Fill a saucepan or wok one-third full of oil, heat to 375°F, or until a cube of bread browns in 30 seconds. Season and dust the fish with flour, dip in the batter, and deep-fry in the oil until golden, about 4–5 minutes.

5

Serve with a spoonful of pea purée and mint vinaigrette.

Chicken and pea shoot salad

Pea shoots, sold in Chinatown stores and increasingly in speciality fruit and vegetable markets, are used in salads and stir-fries. You'll need to perk them up in ice-cold water just before using. Other leaves can be used instead, such as watercress, pousse (baby spinach), or finely sliced uncooked snowpeas. This quick and easy recipe, with its creamy dressing— "spring in a bowl"—is so easy to make.

1 small cooked chicken, preferably poached

3 tablespoons sour cream

2 handfuls pea shoots

4 radishes, sliced

1 cup cherry or baby plum tomatoes, halved

sea salt and freshly ground black pepper

Ginger marinade:

1 garlic clove, crushed

3 tablespoons rice vinegar

juice of 1 lemon

1½ tablespoons superfine sugar

1 whole clove, very finely crushed

2 fresh kaffir lime leaves, very finely chopped (optional)

½ teaspoon chile flakes

1 inch fresh ginger, finely grated, then the juice squeezed from the gratings, solids discarded

Serves 4

Variations:

To make a different dressing, use 3 tablespoons pureéd tofu with ½ tablespoon tahini paste instead of sour cream.

Instead of pea shoots, use other herbs, or a package of herb salad.

Make extra dressing and toss into a salad of steamed rice and fresh cilantro.

1
Remove all the meat from the chicken and pull it into shreds.

2
To make the ginger marinade, put all the ingredients in a large bowl and beat well. Add the chicken and turn to coat well. Chill for at least 1 hour or overnight.

3
Remove the chicken from the marinade. Beat the sour cream into the marinade juices, then add salt and pepper to taste.

4
Carefully fold the chicken with the pea shoots, radishes, and tomatoes, then pile into bowls or onto serving plates. Spoon over the sour cream dressing and serve.

Ham and peas

Many meals can be made from a single ham hock—the flakes of succulent meat and the aromatic saturated stock can be used separately or together to make robust, yet elegant, fare. This is real home cooking, but if you don't want to cook your own ham for the salad variation, use store-bought ham.

1 unsmoked ham hock, about 3 lb.

2 bay leaves

stems of flat-leaf parsley

1 teaspoon dried oregano

2 garlic cloves

1 onion, halved

1 teaspoon freshly grated nutmeg

1 tablespoon peppercorns

3 cups shelled green peas

a handful of cooked and skinned fava beans (optional)

leaves from 1 bunch of mint, torn

sea salt

Roasting mix:

1 tablespoon honey

1 teaspoon sea salt

2 whole cloves, ground

Serves 4

1

Put the ham hock into a deep saucepan and cover with cold water. Add salt and bring to a boil on top of the stove. Skim off the foam and then add the bay leaves, parsley, oregano, garlic, onion, nutmeg, and peppercorns. Cover and simmer gently for 1 hour.

2

Lift the ham from the saucepan and strain the stock. Slash the skin and rub with salt, honey, and ground cloves. Put in a roasting pan and cook in a preheated oven at 425°F for 45 minutes. If it browns too quickly turn the heat down to 400°F.

3

Put the peas and fava beans, if using, in the roasting pan, fill ½ inch deep with ham stock, and cook for 5 minutes. Remove from the oven.

4

Slice the ham and serve hot, with the peas, beans, and mint.

Variation:

This recipe is also good served cold as a pea and ham salad with a parsley and mustard dressing. Beat 2 teaspoons Dijon mustard in a bowl with 2 tablespoons cider vinegar and 3 tablespoons olive oil. Beat in a pinch of sugar, a handful of chopped parsley, some chopped green peppercorns, and 1 crushed garlic clove.
To serve, toss the peas with a chopped shallot, torn mint leaves, and olive oil. Add sliced ham and pour over the dressing.

Herbs inject clean, green flavors into our cooking. Herb shoots in spring—parsley, basil, mint, chives, dill, and cilantro—are soft and delicate at this time of year and should be used simply and as key ingredients. A plate of spaghetti dressed with garlic oil, black pepper, Parmesan, and a mass of chopped basil, or broiled eggplants in virgin olive oil and balsamic vinegar mixed with a bunch of torn mint are testimony to this simplicity—fast, unfussed food with uncomplicated layers of flavor. You can taste the herb. And the food shines.

Herbs come in many flavors, ranging from fragrant dill to citrus-sharp chervil. Mint and basil, especially the aniseed-tasting Thai basil—are good thrown into a lime-juiced salad. So, too, are oriental garlic chives—hot garlicky stems with buds or plain grass-like leaves; both are sold in neat elastic-banded bundles from Thai and Chinese grocers.

Cilantro is a world herb, adding sharp and earthy flavor to food ranging from Mexico and South America to the Middle East and all of Asia (only Japan appears to have turned its back on this "hero" herb). I think it's best uncooked and used full force on food as it is served.

There are so many herbs now to choose from—these days, we're spoilt for choice. You won't get many stems for your money in those flat plastic packages at the supermarket. Your local outdoor market is a better bet for buying herbs by the bundle, for making, say, pesto or salsa verde, where large quantities of the herb are an absolute must.

Herbs that lack luster, with soft leaves or wilted stems, can be brought back to life by submerging them in cold water for half an hour. Shake off excess water and store in a plastic bag in the fridge, not in a jar of water on the window sill—this may brighten up your kitchen, but they won't keep.

A good sharp knife, a chopping board, and a bundle of bushy herbs, and your kitchen will soon be filled with a wonderful aroma—the green green scent of spring.

herbs

Avocado and cilantro toast

Avocado has to be the perfect food—convenient, delicious, and good for you. The dark, warty-skinned Haas variety has the best flavor and texture. It goes well with many herbs, but cilantro is especially good.

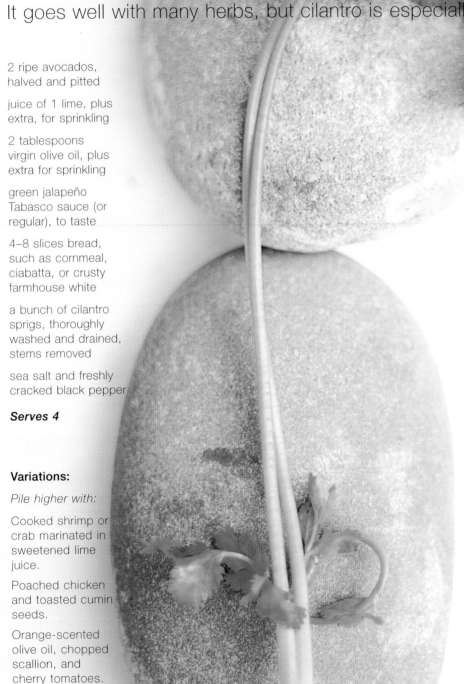

2 ripe avocados, halved and pitted

juice of 1 lime, plus extra, for sprinkling

2 tablespoons virgin olive oil, plus extra for sprinkling

green jalapeño Tabasco sauce (or regular), to taste

4–8 slices bread, such as cornmeal, ciabatta, or crusty farmhouse white

a bunch of cilantro sprigs, thoroughly washed and drained, stems removed

sea salt and freshly cracked black pepper

Serves 4

Variations:

Pile higher with:

Cooked shrimp or crab marinated in sweetened lime juice.

Poached chicken and toasted cumin seeds.

Orange-scented olive oil, chopped scallion, and cherry tomatoes.

1
Using a fork, mash the avocado flesh with the lime juice, 2 tablespoons of the olive oil, the Tabasco, salt, and pepper.

2
Char-grill or toast the bread on both sides and sprinkle with a little salt and extra oil.

3
Spread the avocado thickly over the toast, sprinkle with the remaining olive oil and lime juice, salt, and pepper. Pile cilantro on top.

Basil glass noodles
with shrimp and Thai herbs

Asian basil is a major ingredient in the cooking of Thailand, Vietnam, and Laos. There are several varieties, some used in stir-fries and curries, but the most common ones are used in salads. If you can't find it, use ordinary basil.

6 oz. glass noodles (bean thread vermicelli noodles), about 5 small bundles

a handful of mint sprigs

a handful of Asian basil or sweet basil leaves

3 inches cucumber, peeled, sliced lengthwise, and finely sliced into matchstick julienne strips

Shrimp mixture:

8 oz. cooked peeled shrimp, finely chopped

1 tablespoon peanut satay sauce*

16 canned water chestnuts, drained and finely chopped

1 inch fresh ginger, grated

2 tablespoons finely chopped cilantro leaves

1 tablespoon fish sauce

2 tablespoons lime juice

1 mild red chile, finely diced

Serves 4

Note: Satay sauce is sold in most supermarkets.

1

Put the bean thread vermicelli noodles in a bowl, cover with warm water, and soak until soft, about 15 minutes. Drain, rinse in cold water, and drain again.

2

Put all the ingredients for the shrimp mixture in a small bowl and mix well.

3

Arrange the noodles in 4 bowls. Add small bundles of the mint and basil and strips of cucumber. Divide the shrimp mixture and its juices between the bowls.

4

Toss the noodles with the shrimp mixture as you eat.

Variations:

Add beansprouts or other crunchy stems and leaves to the bowls.

To make a noodle soup with shrimp dumplings: omit the satay from the shrimp mixture and add a drop of beaten egg. Form into balls and sauté until golden. Add these and the herbs to a light chicken stock.

Dilled crayfish with creamy dill caviar

Freshwater crayfish are usually about 4–6 inches long and are a special midsummer feast in Scandinavia. They are always cooked with dill, a favorite herb in Northern Europe. Stems and flowers have a strong aniseed flavor, though the flowers can be hard to find, unless you grow them yourself or buy from a herb grower. If you can't find them, use leaves instead.

24 live freshwater crayfish

4 cups white wine

1 bunch dill

1 leek, halved lengthwise

2 teaspoons coriander seeds

2 tablespoons sea salt

4 heads dill flowers (from florists or your garden), or extra dill

Creamy dill caviar:

1 cup crème fraîche

1 tablespoons finely chopped fresh dill

2 oz. caviar, preferably pink or golden

1 tablespoon lemon juice

Serves 4-8

1

To cook the crayfish, put the wine, dill, leek, coriander seeds, salt, and 4 cups water into a large saucepan and bring to a fast boil.

2

Add the crayfish in batches of 4. Make sure the stock is boiling before each new batch is added. Boil for 6 minutes, then turn off the heat and let cool in the stock.

3

Mix the crème fraîche with the chopped dill, half the caviar and lemon juice, then spoon into small dipping bowls. Top with the remaining caviar and smooth off the top of each bowl with a knife.

4

To serve, put bundles of dill or dill flowers in 4 small bowls, then add a share of the cooked crayfish. Serve the creamy dill caviar separately.

5

To eat, peel the crayfish, dip into the caviar cream and eat with buttered brown bread.

Chile crisp shrimp and garlic chives with wasabi mayonnaise

Garlic chives taste faintly spicy with a garlic-onion flavor and are used here as a salad. You can buy them in bundles from Chinese markets, either as stems with buds, or as narrow reed-like leaves (or use ordinary chives, scallions or wild garlic leaves).

2–3 teaspoons wasabi paste*

4 tablespoons mayonnaise

8 whole uncooked jumbo shrimp

1 stalk lemongrass, trimmed, outer layers discarded, inside layers finely sliced

1 teaspoon chile flakes

2 garlic cloves, chopped

3 teaspoons fish sauce

1 tablespoon lime juice, preferably from kaffir limes

1 teaspoon grated lime zest

1 bunch Chinese garlic chives, some finely scissor-snipped, others left whole

sea salt

corn or peanut oil, for cooking

Serves 4

Note: Wasabi paste (hot Japanese horseradish) is sold in tubes, bottles, or powder form in larger supermarkets and Asian stores.

1

Beat the wasabi and mayonnaise together. Spoon into small dishes.

2

Mix the shrimp with the lemongrass, chile flakes, garlic, fish sauce, lime juice, and zest.

3

Heat 1 tablespoon of the oil in a heavy-based skillet, add the shrimp, and sprinkle generously with sea salt. Sear on both sides until the shells are caramelized and brittle and the flesh opaque.

4

Toss the snipped chives with the shrimp and serve on a bed of whole garlic chives.

5

To eat, remove the head and legs, dip the shrimp into wasabi mayonnaise, and eat them whole, including the crispy shells.

Variations:

Chile crisp shrimp also go with:

Noodles and extra chopped garlic chives.

Stir-fried greens and extra garlic chives.

Salad leaves.

Lemon herb-cured salmon trout with horseradish dilled potatoes

Home curing is easier than you think. Sprinkle the fish with the ingredients, wrap and chill for 2 days. That's all—just remember to start 2 days before you want to eat it. The purple and green tree spinach leaves are often found in supermarket spinach mixes, labeled "red mountain spinach" or orach.

1 salmon or salmon trout, 3 lb., filleted (skin-on)

3 tablespoons sea salt

3 tablespoons sugar

2 teaspoons lemon zest

2 tablespoons akvavit or vodka

1 bunch of dill, chopped

1 bunch of chives, chopped

1 bunch of flat-leaf parsley, chopped

1 bunch of chervil, chopped

1 bunch of basil, chopped

herb leaves, such as purple tree spinach or golden orach, to serve (see recipe introduction)

Herbed potato salad:

2 tablespoons finely chopped red onion

2 tablespoons white wine vinegar

2 teaspoons sugar

2 tablespoons chopped fresh dill

1 tablespoon fresh lemon juice

1 lb. baby new potatoes, boiled and cooled

4 tablespoons sour cream

2 teaspoons freshly grated horseradish

sea salt and freshly ground black pepper

Serves 4

1

Put the fillets, skin side down, on a large piece of plastic wrap. Remove any pin bones (they run down the lateral line). Mix the salt, sugar, lemon zest, akvavit or vodka, dill, chives, parsley, chervil, and basil in a bowl, then press onto the flesh. Wrap tightly in plastic, put on a shallow tray, and weigh down. Refrigerate for 1 day, then turn it over and refrigerate again. After 2 days, unwrap and rinse off the curing ingredients with cold running water. Pat dry with paper towels. Cover with more finely chopped herbs, then wrap in plastic until just before serving.

2

To make the potato salad, put the onion in a bowl with the wine vinegar, sugar, dill, lemon juice, salt, and pepper. Marinate for 20 minutes, then add the potatoes, sour cream, and horseradish. Serve in 1 large or 4 small bowls.

3

Finely slice the salmon crosswise into strips, leaving the skin behind. Serve on a bed of leaves.

Herb and fava bean falafels

Falafels are the pride of Lebanese cooking, starring favorite Middle Eastern herbs like mint, parsley, and cilantro. Don't be discouraged by the long list of ingredients—this recipe is very simple.

1 cup podded fava beans

1 cup chickpeas (garbanzo beans), soaked overnight in cold water to cover, or 1 cup canned chickpeas, rinsed well in cold water

3 garlic cloves, crushed

4 scallions, chopped

1 heaped tablespoon chopped parsley

1 heaped tablespoon chopped cilantro

1 heaped tablespoon chopped dill

1 heaped tablespoon chopped mint

3 teaspoons ground coriander

3 teaspoons ground cumin and 1 teaspoon cumin seeds, pan-toasted

3–4 tablespoons olive oil

1 tablespoon lemon juice

1 teaspoon baking powder mixed with 2 tablespoons warm water

4 tablespoons sesame seeds, half pan-toasted, half plain

sea salt and freshly ground black pepper

4 warmed pita breads, to serve (optional)

vegetable oil, for frying

1

Put the fava beans, chickpeas, garlic, scallions, herbs, coriander, cumin, olive oil, lemon juice, and baking powder mixture in a food processor and process to a coarse paste. Add salt and pepper to taste. Chill.

2

Roll the falafel mixture into walnut-sized balls. Roll one third of the balls in the plain sesame seeds and another third in the toasted sesame seeds. Leave the remainder plain. Heat the oil in a skillet, saucepan, or wok and gently sauté or deep-fry the falafels until golden. Drain on crumpled paper towels.

3

To make the salad, put the yogurt, lemon juice, tahini paste, salt, and pepper in a bowl and beat with a fork. Add the salad leaves, herbs, cucumber, and radish and toss gently.

4

Serve the falafels with the salad on plates or in warm pita bread.

Herb and radish salad:

4 tablespoons plain yogurt

1 teaspoon lemon juice

1 teaspoon tahini paste

assorted salad leaves and herbs, such as mizuna, golden orach, mint, and cilantro

5 cm cucumber, finely sliced

4–6 radishes, finely sliced

sea salt and freshly ground black pepper

Serves 4

Parma chicken kiev

with peas, fava beans, mint, and basil

The first tender, delicious shoots of mint, basil, and chives appear in early spring, and are used in the kiev stuffing for these chicken "hams"—perfect for a light lunch or dinner. Boning the chicken legs is a little complicated, but easier than you might think—and they can also be prepared ahead.

¾ cup soft butter

3 garlic cloves, crushed

4 tablespoons finely chopped parsley

2 tablespoons finely chopped basil

4 chicken legs, skinned, foot joint removed, then boned*

8 thin slices Parma ham

2 cups shelled fresh green peas

2 cups shelled fresh fava beans

2 cups yellow wax beans or green beans

1 handful of fresh mint leaves

1 handful of fresh basil leaves

1 bunch of fresh chives

sea salt and freshly ground black pepper

olive oil, for brushing

Serves 4

Note: To bone the legs, start from the "hip," separating the meat from the bone with the tip of a sharp knife. Follow the bone, keeping the flesh intact until you reach the "knee." Roll back the flesh and carefully scrape the meat from around the cartilage— don't worry about making a few holes. Proceed half way down the next bone, fold back the meat and cut off the bone. A small "handle" of bone will remain. (Your butcher may do this job for you.)

1

Mash the butter with the garlic, parsley, basil, salt, and pepper. Stuff into the leg cavities and cover the openings with the loose flap of flesh. Wrap 2 overlapping slices of Parma ham around each leg and stand them upright on in oiled roasting pan. (It can be prepared to this point, wrapped in plastic, refrigerated overnight, then cooked the next day.)

2

Brush the chicken with oil and roast in a preheated oven at 425°F for 25 minutes or until crisp. Pierce with the point of a sharp knife: the juices will run clear when the chicken is done.

3

Simmer the peas and beans in boiling salted water until al dente, about 4 minutes. Drain and mix in the herbs.

4

To serve, put one Parma chicken kiev in each bowl or plate, surround with the peas, beans, and leaves of mint, basil, and chives. Pour over the caramelized juices from the roasting pan, then serve.

Rhubarb—you either love it or loathe it. I think it's great—big, strong, and bold in taste, color, and stature. Some would say brash, especially those forced bright pink stems. This is early rhubarb that has been grown in vast, blacked-out polytunnels producing forced stems that, as they grow, are banished from the light of day. This keeps them tender and chlorophyll-free (they are pure pink) and therefore much sweeter than the outdoor garden-grown rhubarb—the deep pink to ruby red and green stalks of late spring and summer.

In the black stillness of the polytunnel, if you stand perfectly still, it is said that you can hear a faint rustle, as the rhubarb stretches and unfurls its pale, unformed leaf tips in search of the light it will never find. Sounds a sad tale. Although I like forced rhubarb, I actually prefer the more robust outdoor stems. They have a more characterful flavor (perhaps because they've had a happier life), although they will need more sugar to sweeten them. They also need vigorous trimming and should be cut into 1–1½-inch lengths before cooking. They then turn to anything from a beautiful pastel mauve-pink to red-brown or deep scarlet and exude plenty of perfumed juice. They look less refined, but taste more gutsy than their more effete cousins.

Rhubarb originated in northern Asia and was grown for its beauty and medicinal properties until it was discovered by European cooks in the eighteenth century. And what a happy discovery—a huge bundle cooks down to a smooth soft consistency in a matter of minutes.

One important point is that you should never, ever eat the leaves—they're poisonous. This isn't a problem when you buy rhubarb—the leaves are always removed—but if you grow your own, take care.

But—even if you don't eat rhubarb, you'll love the look of it— a large vase full of shocking pink stems on your kitchen bench will look truly spectacular.

(It could catch on!)

rhubarb

Rosewater-poached rhubarb
with vanilla ricotta

Delicate poached stems of rhubarb bobbing in rose-scented juice are served with soft vanilla-flavoured cheese.

10 oz. rhubarb, cut into
bite-sized chunks

½ cup sugar

a squeeze of lemon juice

1 tablespoon rosewater

2 cups ricotta cheese

1 vanilla bean, split lengthwise

½ tablespoon superfine sugar

2 tablespoons heavy cream

Serves 4

1

To cook the rhubarb, put the sugar, lemon juice, and ½ cup water into a saucepan, stir, and bring to a boil. Turn down the heat and simmer gently until all the sugar has dissolved. Add the chunks of rhubarb and stir again to coat. Simmer for about 3 minutes. Gently turn over the rhubarb, cover the pan with a lid, turn off the heat, stir in the rosewater, and let cool.

2

Using a wooden spoon, press the ricotta through a sieve into a bowl. Scrape the seeds from the vanilla bean into the ricotta and mix well. Dissolve the sugar in the cream and beat into the ricotta. Chill.

3

Spoon the rhubarb and rosewater juices into bowls or onto small serving plates and serve with the vanilla ricotta in spoonfuls, or in a separate bowl.

Iced rhubarb lassi

Almond milk, rhubarb, ice, and thick yogurt make a sublime lassi (Indian yogurt drink). Prepare double quantities of each and keep refrigerated: at the flick of a switch you'll have the lot blended into shape. Good enough—if not too good—for dessert.

7 oz. rhubarb, chopped

2 tablespoons sugar

1½ cups ground almonds

1 cinnamon stick

2 cups milk

2¾ cups plain yogurt

about 1 cup crushed ice

strawberries or strawberry syrup, to serve (optional)

Serves 4

Note: *The line of red strawberry juice was made by simmering strawberries with sugar and a little lemon juice, sieving the juice, and reducing it to a syrup. Teaspoons of the juice were trickled down inside the glasses before filling them with lassi.*

1

Put the rhubarb in a saucepan, add 3 tablespoons water and the sugar, bring to a boil, then simmer until soft, about 8 minutes. Purée in a blender or food processor. Chill.

2

Put the ground almonds, cinnamon, and milk in a saucepan and warm through. Set aside to infuse until cool. Strain the almond milk through a fine-meshed sieve and squeeze out as much of milk as possible. Discard the cinnamon and residue. Chill.

3

Put the rhubarb, almond milk, yogurt, and ice in a blender or food processor and blend well. Taste, add sugar if necessary, then serve.

Rhubarb and custard pastries

Rhubarb and custard is a favorite combination, but put them on a pastry with a sprinkling of soft almonds and you're really up there on Cloud Nine in Taste Heaven. You can cheat a little if you like and buy ready-made custard, but making your own is so easy it's worth trying.

5 stalks young rhubarb, cut in 2-inch lengths

2 tablespoons sugar

1 vanilla bean, split lengthwise

1¼ cups milk

⅔ cup heavy cream

4 large egg yolks

6 tablespoons superfine sugar

2 tablespoons all-purpose flour

1 package frozen puff pastry (1 lb.), thawed

1 tablespoon chopped blanched almonds

confectioner's sugar, for dusting

Serves 4

1

Spread the rhubarb across a wide saucepan in a single layer, sprinkle with the sugar, and add about 3 tablespoons water. Heat to simmering, carefully turn over the slices, turn off the heat and cover with a lid—the rhubarb should be poached through and tender. Let cool.

2

Put the split vanilla bean, milk, and cream in a saucepan and bring to a boil. Remove from the heat.

3

Beat 3 of the egg yolks, sugar, and flour in a bowl until thick and pale. Slowly beat in the hot vanilla milk (discard the bean). Pour the custard back into the milk pan and cook very gently, stirring all the time, for about 1 minute—don't let it boil, or it will curdle. Remove from the heat.

4

Roll out the puff pastry to ¼ inch thick and cut into small square shapes or a long rectangle. Spread custard over the top, leaving a ¼-inch edge of pastry uncovered. Top with lines of rhubarb, push the nuts into the pastry, and brush with the remaining egg yolk, beaten. Dust with confectioner's sugar and bake in a preheated oven at 400°F for 20 minutes for small pastries or 30 minutes if large—or until puffed and golden.

5

Dust with more confectioner's sugar and serve warm.

Rhubarb fool with meringues

To save time, buy meringues from a local bakery, but if you want small ones with marshmallow-soft centers, you'll have to make them yourself. Remember they need a couple of hours or so in a very cool oven—so plan ahead.

1 lb. rhubarb, chopped

4 tablespoons superfine sugar

1 egg

1 cup mascarpone cheese

½ cup heavy cream

Meringues:

3 egg whites

¾ cup superfine sugar

Serves 4

Variations:

Sandwich the fool between two large meringues or sandwich between layers of sponge cake.

Instead of meringue, serve with amaretti or shortbread cookies dusted with confectioner's sugar.

1

Put the rhubarb into a saucepan, add 3 tablespoons of the sugar and about 3 tablespoons water, then cook until soft.

2

Beat the egg in a bowl with the remaining sugar, then add the mascarpone and 2 tablespoons of the cream and beat again.

3

Whip the remaining cream until it forms soft peaks, then barely fold the cream and rhubarb into the mascarpone mixture, to form a marbled effect. Spoon into bowls or glasses and chill well.

4

To make the meringues, beat the egg whites with an electric beater until stiff. Still beating, gradually shower in half the sugar, then gently fold in the remainder.

5

Put a sheet of parchment paper on a baking tray. Using 2 spoons, shape spoonfuls of meringue and arrange in a line across the tray. Bake in the oven at 200°F for about 2–3 hours, depending how soft you like the meringues to be in the centers.

6

Serve the fools on a plate with the meringues.

Buttermilk crêpes

with ginger rhubarb jam and soft cheese

This adaptable sweet-savory ginger rhubarb jam can also be served on warmed biscuits or on buttered toast with thick cream or crème fraîche. Alternatively, cook with a tablespoon of raspberry vinegar and serve as a relish with roast duck or other game birds.

Ginger rhubarb jam:

1 lb. rhubarb, chopped

1 cup brown sugar

1 teaspoon ground allspice

grated zest and juice of 3 oranges, preferably blood oranges

1 inch fresh ginger, thickly sliced

3 tablespoons superfine sugar

soft cheese, such as robiola, o serve

Buttermilk crêpes:

⅔ cup all-purpose flour

a pinch of salt

2 eggs

1 tablespoon superfine sugar

1 cup buttermilk

butter, for cooking

Serves 4

1

To make the ginger rhubarb jam, put 14 oz. of the rhubarb in a saucepan, add the brown sugar, allspice, the juice of 1 orange, and the ginger. Stew for about 30 minutes, stirring regularly. Remove the ginger and stir in the remaining rhubarb. Let cool.

2

Put the orange zest, superfine sugar, and remaining orange juice in a saucepan, bring to a boil, and reduce to a syrup. Set aside to keep warm.

3

To make the crêpes, put the flour and salt in a bowl. Make a well in the center, add the eggs and sugar, then beat slowly to incorporate the flour. Slowly beat in the buttermilk to make a smooth batter, then thin further with ½ cup water.

4

Brush a non-stick skillet with butter, swirl in a large spoonful of batter, and cook until golden, 1–2 minutes on each side. Repeat until all the mixture is used. As they are cooked, transfer to a warm plate, stack each crêpe between sheets of waxed paper, and keep them warm.

5

Spread the crêpes with rhubarb jam, add a slice of cheese, roll up, and pour over a little orange syrup.

Rhubarb
with vine raisins and brie

This is such a simple dish it hardly needs a recipe. If you can't find muscatel raisins on the vine, use ordinary plump California raisins instead. This cheese should always be served at room temperature.

1 quantity poached rhubarb (page 72, step 1)

1 medium or 4 small ripe brie, or soft cow's milk cheese with a rind

4 sprigs dried raisins on the vine

Serves 4

1

Put the poached rhubarb in a bowl and set on a small plate.

2

Set the raisins beside the bowl, mix them with the rhubarb, or dot them over the whole cheese, then serve. (If you leave the raisins on the cheese, covered, for a few hours they soften and plump up until light and perfect. Don't soak them.)

3

If using the whole cheese, serve with a small spoon for dipping the soft cheese out of the center.

index